The Other Mozart

The Life *of the* Famous Chevalier de Saint-George

Hugh Brewster Illustrated by Eric Velasquez

Abrams Books for Young Readers

New York

"It's a boy, a fine, fine boy!"

The midwife held up the bawling baby and a smile crossed Nanon's exhausted face. It was Christmas Day, 1745, on the French island of Guadeloupe in the West Indies. Outside the plantation house, the sounds of holiday drumming and dancing came from the street of the slave cabins.

"He should be called Joseph," the local priest decreed. "That's the name for a boy born on Christmas Day." But the priest did not write the baby's name in the parish record book. Although Joseph's father was a wealthy planter from a prominent French family, his mother, Nanon, was a slave. And the children of slaves were not registered by the church.

But Georges de Bologne-Saint-George loved the baby son that Nanon had given him. When Joseph grew older, his father would sometimes put him on his saddle when he rode out to inspect the work on the plantations. In the sugarcane fields Joseph heard the songs of Africa. One worker would start the singing as he worked and the others would join in, repeating the tunes over and over. On Sundays and feast days, the Africans danced to their own music. The children danced as well, imitating the moves of the adults. Joseph would bring them little cakes his mother had made. Sometimes, he, too, would sway to the rhythm of the drumming and singing.

Joseph also loved to tap his feet when Monsieur Platon played his fiddle.

Monsieur Platon helped Joseph's father manage the plantation but he was also a good fiddler who had once played in the cafés of Paris. When Joseph was old enough, Monsieur Platon gave him lessons on the violin. Georges de Bologne-Saint-George wanted his son to be educated like a gentleman. So Joseph learned to read and write in French. He also learned how to ride and shoot. And his father taught him some of the basics of fencing with a small dueling sword.

But Joseph would soon say good-bye to Monsieur Platon and to the island of Guadeloupe. When Joseph was eight, his father announced that he was selling his plantations to go and live in France. Nanon and Joseph would go with him. They would live in a fine house in Paris!

RIGHT: Joseph's father owned two sugarcane plantations on Guadeloupe. When the crop was ready for harvesting, African workers would cut sugarcane stalks and load them onto wagons. Oxen then hauled the cane stalks to the sugar mill where they were crushed between huge rollers. The cane juice flowed into gutters that led to the boiling house. There it was boiled down into a thick syrup that crystallized into sugar.

This painting depicts the River Seine in Paris much as Joseph and Nanon would have seen it. The river was the heart of the city and goods arrived daily on barges to be sold in markets along the banks. People also bathed, did laundry, and watered horses in the river. The towers of the medieval cathedral of Notre Dame can be seen to the left. The Notre Dame Bridge, at center, has houses built right across it.

As Nanon boarded the sailing ship, the captain bowed and welcomed her on board. People had always remarked on how beautiful Nanon was. And in the stylish silk gown that Georges had bought for her, she looked lovelier than ever. Georges had also taken the necessary steps with the authorities to make sure that his son and Nanon were no longer slaves. In France, slavery had been outlawed—though it still existed in French colonies such as Guadeloupe where planters made fortunes from slave labor.

When their ship arrived at the French port of Bordeaux, Joseph looked over the rail at the fine houses and warehouses that lined the bustling wharves. The slave trade, and goods from the colonies harvested by slaves, had helped to make Bordeaux a prosperous town.

From Bordeaux they traveled by horse-drawn coach to Paris, where Georges's brother had found a house for them on a fashionable square. As Joseph and Nanon explored their new city, people on the street often stared at them. There were not many African faces in Paris in 1753, and none as elegantly dressed as this regal black woman and her handsome young son.

In Paris, status was everything. To be rich was important but being an aristocrat was the best of all. Georges knew his son would not find it easy to be accepted in snobbish French society. Before leaving the Caribbean, he created a title for him. His son's new name would be Joseph Bologne, the Chevalier de Saint-George. (A *chevalier* in France was equal to a knight in England, where he would have been called Sir Joseph.) And since Georges had an important new job as an official of the king's court, he could stare down anyone who questioned his son's right to the title of Chevalier.

Georges was also determined that Joseph would excel in all the pastimes of a young chevalier. When he turned thirteen, Joseph was sent to board at one of France's finest fencing academies run by a master swordsman named La Boëssière. In the mornings, the boys learned mathematics, history, and languages as well as music, art, and dance. Horsemanship was taught on the grounds of the nearby Tuileries Palace.

The afternoons were given over to fencing—a skill at which every young aristocrat had to excel.

Within a few years, Joseph was the best fencer in the school. It helped that he was taller than most Frenchmen. But he was also very strong and agile. Swordsmen were eager to challenge him and crowds came to see "the Negro" (as he was called) duel.

Once Joseph heard a young aristocrat make snide remarks about having to fence with a "half-caste." The usually gentle Joseph picked him up and threw him across the room where he landed with a crash! During another match, a young noble who didn't want to compete against Joseph kept retreating and would never attack. Frustrated, Joseph lifted him up, turned him upside down, and carried him around the hall—to the cheers of the spectators.

ABOVE AND LEFT: *At La Boëssière's school, Joseph was taught proper fencing form as shown in these illustrations from books of the period. He learned how to fence with a light, flexible sword known as a foil. The thin blade of the foil had a blunt tip, as the goal was to hit, or* touche, *one's opponent, not to cause injury. (La Boëssière, in fact, invented one of the first protective facemasks in fencing.) Swords were no longer used for combat in France but fencing was a highly prized pastime for gentlemen. La Boëssière's son became a lifelong friend of Joseph's and later wrote, "Perhaps the most extraordinary man ever known in fencing was the famous Saint-George."*

The young ladies of Paris had never met a chevalier like Joseph. He was a famous athlete, yet he was also kind, and with fine manners.

And he always had a ready smile. One admirer described his teeth as "two rows of pearls set on black velvet."

It is believed that one young woman won his heart. They likely met at a weekend party in a country chateau where they danced together and rode horses and took long walks. When the girl's family found out about the romance, they sent her away from Paris. Joseph never saw his first love again until he watched from behind a pillar as she climbed the church steps to marry another man, who was white.

Joseph would never marry—though he would always be a favorite with the ladies. He later wrote a song with the words,

Oh the joy of being loved tenderly,
And yet what disappointment follows in its wake!

RIGHT: Joseph was a popular guest at parties like this one, held in the grand houses of the wealthy. His father's high position at the king's court assured him a place on the best invitation lists. Joseph was also a nimble dancer and was much sought after as a partner by the young ladies of Paris. "Lively, supple, and slender, he astonished everyone with his agility," is how La Boëssière's son described him. "Everyone agreed that if he had devoted himself to the ballet, he would have done amazing things." Although the young women of Joseph's circle were charmed by him, their families would never permit marriage to "the Negro," as he was known. His friends and admirers preferred to call him "the American" since to them he was a breath of fresh air from the New World.

By the age of only twenty, Joseph was the best fencer in France. He could flick off an opponent's shirt button with a twist of his sword. The newspapers called him "the famous Saint-George," and all Paris loved to talk of his exploits.

"Did you hear that the famous Saint-George has swum across the River Seine with one arm tied behind his back—on an icy January day?"

"I heard he danced till dawn at the masked ball given by the Duc de Chartres!"

"The newspaper says the famous Saint-George won Sunday's carriage race on the Champs-Elysées! He was driving the *cabriolet* his father bought him for defeating the master swordsman Picard from Rouen!"

"Ah yes, but what about the Italian, Faldoni? Will Saint-George dare to fight him?"

Faldoni, Faldoni, Faldoni... In the summer of 1766, Joseph was tired of hearing about Faldoni, the Italian champion who had come to Paris to challenge him. But as Faldoni defeated one famous fencer after another, the pressure grew for a duel with Saint-George. Joseph knew the Italian was a much more experienced fencer than he was. But finally, he agreed to a match. The date was set for the eighth of September and for days beforehand, Paris talked of nothing else—even members of the royal court were planning to attend!

LEFT: "[Saint-George] is the most accomplished man in Europe in Riding, Running, Shooting, Fencing, Dancing, Music," wrote future U.S. President John Adams in his diary on May 17, 1779. Adams would become the second president of the United States in 1797. But in 1779, he was in Paris to enlist France's help during the American Revolution. He had heard much about Joseph and wrote that he could "hit the button, any button, on the coat of the greatest [fencing] masters. He will hit a Crown Piece [coin] with a pistol ball."

Finally, the great day came,
and a huge crowd waited hours for the fencing match to begin. When the two duelists appeared and saluted each other, the cheers of "Bravo Saint-George!" were long and loud.

When Joseph made the first hit, or *touche*, the crowd went wild. Faldoni then began a furious advance. Joseph skillfully blocked, or *parried*, each expert thrust. But then the Italian made a sudden darting move—and scored. Before long, Faldoni touched again!

Joseph soon evened up the score but Faldoni matched him with yet another swift move and touched for a third time. Joseph realized that the older man's experience would make him hard to beat. He tried attacking with some of his famous, powerful thrusts but the Italian cleverly parried each one of them. After a long and furious fight, Faldoni was declared the winner with four touches to Joseph's two.

This was Joseph's first defeat, a very public one, and he took it hard. Faldoni praised Joseph and said that at the age of only twenty he could still become the best fencer in Europe. Later, Nanon tried to comfort him with similar words. But Joseph still felt humiliated. He brooded for a while and then he reached a decision. He decided to show Paris that fencing wasn't the only thing at which he could excel.

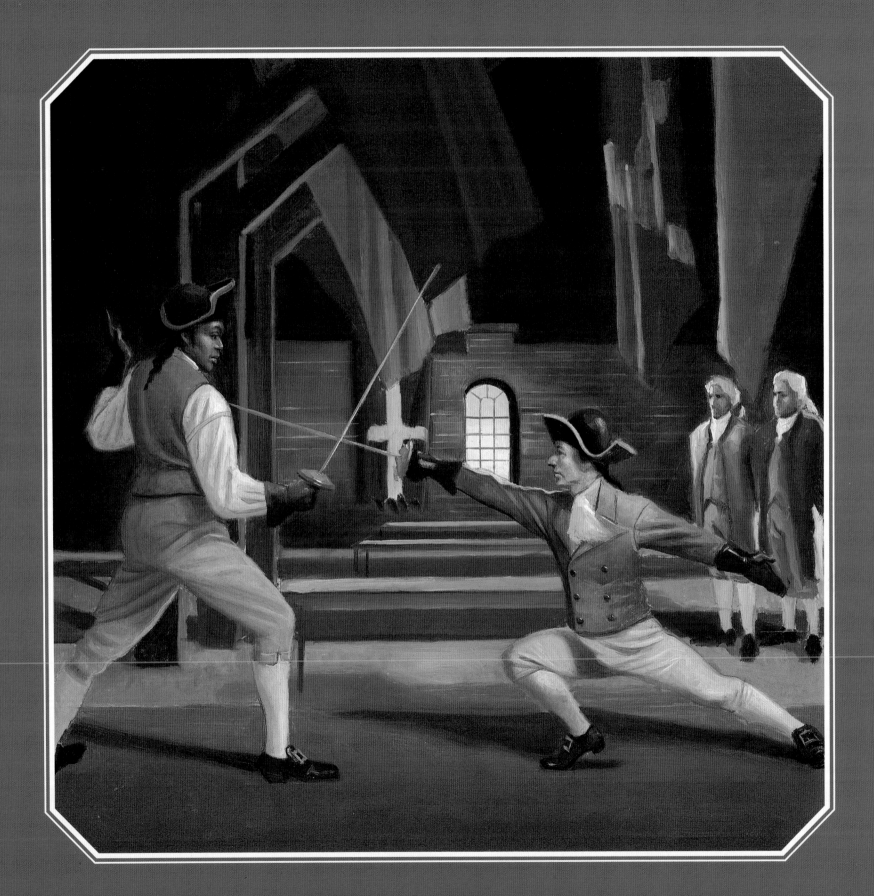

Most gentlemen were expected to be able to play a musical instrument—but Joseph had more talent than most gentlemen. His violin lessons from Monsieur Platon had been a good start but now he studied with the best musicians in Paris.

Before long, people were talking about how the famous Saint-George could duel with a violin bow as well as a sword. At parties in grand houses, he would be invited to show off his skills. Joseph would make his violin imitate the sounds of the birds of the tropics. His fingers would dance on the strings as he played swooping runs and dazzling trills. When he finished, his audience would pause, stunned, and then burst into cheers.

In 1769, Joseph became the first violinist of the largest orchestra in Paris. And three years later, the orchestra performed two violin concertos that he had composed. A newspaper review said that the Chevalier de Saint-George received "the most rapturous applause"—both for his playing and for his compositions. The next year, at the age of just twenty-four, Joseph became the orchestra's conductor.

RIGHT: A musical group performs at an elegant tea party in the home of a French prince in 1766. The pianist is the ten-year-old Wolfgang Amadeus Mozart—already a famous musician. It was at musical gatherings like this one that Joseph made his reputation as a violinist, playing an instrument similar to the one shown above. But Joseph also liked to play for the ordinary people who had cheered for him as a swordsman. On summer evenings, he would sometimes play outdoors in parks and large crowds would gather around him.

One morning in 1774, Joseph received a special envelope. It had a wax seal with the royal crest stamped on it. France's new young queen, Marie Antoinette, had heard of the renowned Saint-George. Would he come to the palace to play music with her?

A few days later, Joseph stood before the gilded gates of the palace of Versailles. After crossing the vast cobblestoned courtyard, a uniformed servant led him down the famous Hall of Mirrors past buzzing knots of courtiers waiting to see the king. As he passed the hall's huge mirrors, he saw his strong, athletic figure in a white satin vest and pearl-gray velvet breeches reflected over and over again.

Finally, Joseph was ushered into an elegant music room with golden nymphs painted on the ceiling. There the queen sat surrounded by her ladies-in-waiting. Marie Antoinette was only nineteen, but to Joseph she seemed even younger. When she raised her hand to stifle a giggle, the diamonds in her swept-up hairdo would twinkle and her large earrings would shimmer. But when they played together, Joseph discovered that the queen was quite a good musician. And she liked the handsome chevalier. Before leaving the palace, Joseph was told that the queen would be pleased to receive him at Versailles more often.

No doubt Joseph described each visit he made to Versailles to his mother. And when he told her that he had met the King of France—and that he was a rather fat and dull-looking man in a powdered wig, not the regal king he had imagined—Nanon must have laughed and laughed.

LEFT: Marie Antoinette plays the harp to an audience of courtiers at Versailles. It would have been in a room like this one that the young queen received Joseph. She may have accompanied him on the harpsichord while he played the violin. Music was one of Marie Antoinette's great passions. She had been raised in the imperial court in Vienna, the musical capital of Europe, and all the great musicians of the day came to perform for her family. She learned to play several instruments and, as queen of France, supported the work of composers and musicians.

The Queen of Versailles

Marie Antoinette was not her real name. And although she was the queen of France, she was not French. She had been born Maria Antonia, the eighth daughter (and twelfth child) of Empress Maria Theresa, the powerful ruler of the Austrian empire. The Austrian empress considered her daughters to be "sacrifices to politics." Their purpose in life was to become the wives of foreign princes or kings whose countries would then be closely tied to her empire.

At the age of only thirteen, Maria Antonia was told that she was to be married to Prince Louis-Auguste, the heir to the throne of France. Soon French tutors arrived at the palace in Vienna to teach her how to walk, talk, and behave like a French crown princess, or *dauphine*. For over a year, she wondered what her future husband would look like. When she finally saw a portrait of Louis-Auguste, she hoped that he would be better looking than the plain, pudgy boy in the picture!

Marie Antoinette as the young Dauphine of France

April 21, 1770 The French king sends a satin-lined coach and dozens of horsemen to Vienna to bring the empress's daughter to France. The journey takes over two weeks because of the celebrations held at every stop. At the French border, Maria Antonia enters a small wooden palace built especially for her arrival. There, she changes out of her Austrian clothes into a splendid French gown. When she reappears, the crowd cheers loudly for the new Dauphine of France, Marie Antoinette.

May 16, 1770 Marie Antoinette, aged fourteen, and the sixteen-year-old Louis-Auguste are married in the chapel at the palace of Versailles. She had met her husband-to-be only three days before the wedding. The portrait hadn't lied—he wasn't her Prince Charming. Nevertheless, during the ceremony, the Dauphine looked radiant in a gown of white brocade.

May 30, 1770 Marie Antoinette and her new husband attend a huge fireworks display held in their honor in Paris. Afterward, the crowds stampede and 133 people are trampled to death.

Benjamin Franklin is received at the French court in 1778

July 1774 The king gives his wife a special gift—a small palace on the grounds of Versailles called the Petit Trianon. There, Marie Antoinette can escape from the prying eyes of the court and entertain her own friends. Around her little palace she creates elaborate gardens with lakes and grottoes and Greek temples. She even builds a miniature farm and country village called *Le Hameau.*

October 27, 1776 Benjamin Franklin sets sail for France as a representative of the American Continental Congress. His mission is to persuade the French to help the rebellious American colonies in their fight for independence from Great Britain.

February 5, 1778 France signs a treaty of alliance with the Americans and Franklin is invited to meet the king and queen. Crowds shout "*Vive* [Long live] Franklin!" as his carriage passes through the gates of Versailles. Over the next three years, more than 44,000 French sailors and soldiers will fight with General George Washington in the American War of Independence.

June–July, 1770 Louis-Auguste spends most of his time hunting on horseback and ignoring his new wife. The court gossips chatter endlessly about this. Over 3,000 French aristocrats live at Versailles and they have little to do except seek favors, trade rumors, and plot. Marie Antoinette finds the court's formality suffocating and it seems that everything she does is wrong.

August 1770 During a stay at the private royal retreat at Marly, Louis and Marie Antoinette finally have time to get to know each other. But it is almost three years before he is able to be truly affectionate to her and eight years before their first child is born.

May 10, 1774 King Louis XV dies and his grandson, Louis-Auguste, becomes King Louis XVI. At his coronation, the French people cheer the new young king and queen and hope that life will be better during their reign.

December 19, 1778 Marie Antoinette gives birth to a baby girl, not the male heir to the throne that everyone had hoped for. She is named Marie Thérèse. In 1781, she gives birth to a boy, Louis Joseph. A second son is born in 1785, and another daughter in 1786 who only lives for eleven months. In 1789, her first son, the *Dauphin*, dies at the age of seven. Lost in grief over the death of their son, the king and queen do not notice the black storm clouds gathering over their kingdom.

ABOVE: *The elaborate interior of the Royal Opera House at Versailles is shown in this ink sketch done in 1770. I* *depicts a performance of an opera called* Athalie *that was put on as part of the celebrations in honor of the marriage of the Dauphin, the future King Louis XVI, to Marie Antoinette. To become the director of this opera house would*

By 1775, Joseph was a celebrated violinist, conductor, and composer. Surely, he was the perfect person to become the director of the Royal Opera—the highest musical post in the land. Marie Antoinette encouraged the king to appoint her favorite music partner, the brilliant young chevalier.

But jealous courtiers said, "How could the king have a Negro as head of his opera house? Surely there is a Frenchman better qualified!" Then three divas who were stars of the Opera wrote a letter to the king. They claimed it would be "scandalous" if they were "made subject to the orders of a mulatto."

This news frustrated the king. He said that if Saint-George was not to be head of the opera then neither would anyone else! So the post was left unfilled and the opera was run by one of the king's courtiers.

This was a humiliating blow for Joseph. But, as with Faldoni, he would not be beaten by it. He would show the world that he could create his own operas.

LEFT: Louis XVI, unlike his wife, was not a great lover of music. So when Marie Antoinette proposed that Joseph become the new head of the Royal Opera, the king was willing to accept her advice. But Louis was a shy, awkward man who hated nothing more than a fuss within his court. And the news of Joseph's possible appointment created lots of angry talk at Versailles. The two opera singers and one dancer who signed the letter of protest to the king had other motives. All three of them were fading talents. They knew that Joseph would likely replace them with new performers once he was in charge. Although Joseph did not get the post he deserved, the controversy made many people in France ask for the first time, "Could a black person be just as talented as a white one?" It also made Joseph throw himself into writing more of his own music and striving to become an opera composer.

A year and a half later, Saint-George's first opera, *Ernestine*, was performed in Paris. But it flopped! The critics said the problem was the story—not the music. And they hoped that Saint-George would continue to compose music for the stage. So Joseph found another playwright and created *La Chasse* (The Hunt)—which was a hit! Parisians flocked to buy tickets. Four days after it opened, Joseph received another special envelope with the royal crest stamped on it. Inside was a message from the king. His Majesty wanted *La Chasse* to be performed for his invited guests at the palace of Marly.

Marly was the king's private retreat in the country—a small, elegant palace surrounded by sumptuous gardens. Only *la crème de la crème* were invited to Marly. Even as the director of the Royal Opera, Joseph might never have made it to Marly.

On the night of the performance, Joseph took his place at the front of the orchestra and bowed to the king and queen and the glittering assembly of guests. He raised his arms and the overture began. *La Chasse* was a comedy and the audience laughed and applauded in all the right places. At the end, they cheered Joseph and his singers. Joseph bowed to the audience and to the king and queen. As Marie Antoinette nodded graciously in return, the diamonds in her hair sparkled more brightly than ever.

When Joseph described this evening to Nanon, she must surely have thought about how far they had come from the sugarcane fields of the Caribbean.

RIGHT: Marie Antoinette helped turn a performance of Joseph's first opera, Ernestine, *into a disaster. One character in the opera was a country bumpkin who called out the greeting "Ohé!" (pronounced "O-aay") in a yodeling voice. The queen was very amused by this and every time he came on stage she cried out "O-aay" and clapped her hands. Soon the rest of the audience began shouting out "O-aay" as well, until the whole opera became ridiculous. Fights even broke out in the audience. After the curtain fell, the queen was heard calling to her coachman outside the theater, "To Versailles! O-aay!" After this,* Ernestine *was rarely performed again.*

Joseph would write three more successful operas. And he kept on writing concertos and sonatas for the orchestra as well.

The name Saint-George was often seen on concert posters around Paris beside famous names like Wolfgang Amadeus Mozart. People even called Joseph *"le Mozart noir"*—the black Mozart.

But the most famous composer in all of Europe was Franz-Josef Haydn. Musicians affectionately called him "Papa" Haydn. In 1785, Joseph traveled to Vienna to meet the great man. Two years later, Joseph conducted the first performances of six symphonies that Haydn had composed especially for his orchestra. Today these are known as Haydn's "Paris" Symphonies. The fourth one is called *La Reine* (The Queen) as it was Marie Antoinette's favorite.

RIGHT: Musicians of Saint-George's day perform at a special occasion. Joseph always insisted that the players in his orchestra be as elegantly dressed as he was. He believed they should be as fine to behold as they were to hear. Many of his players were amateurs who played for the love of it. The only jobs for professional musicians in the 1700s were within wealthy households. And there, they were considered to be servants. Mozart himself complained that as a music director for a wealthy patron, his rank was higher than a cook but lower than a butler!

Haydn and Mozart

RIGHT: The "Paris" Symphonies that Joseph Haydn wrote for Saint-George to conduct in 1787 are only six of the 108 symphonies that Haydn wrote during his long life. He also composed hundreds of string quartets, trios, piano sonatas, operas, and works for choir and orchestra. All from a man who had to teach himself music! He was born in 1732 to a poor family in a small Austrian village. As a young choirboy, his good singing voice took him to the cathedral choir and school in Vienna. But when his voice changed, he was expelled! As a teenager, Haydn had to support himself with odd jobs. But in his spare time, he studied the works of noted composers and read books about musical theory. Eventually, he began writing his own compositions and working as a conductor. When he died in 1809 at the age of seventy-seven, he had become one of the greatest composers of his time and had been a friend and mentor to both Mozart and Beethoven.

OPPOSITE: Wolfgang Amadeus Mozart had been a famous musician in Europe since he was a child. At the age of five, he could play the harpsichord brilliantly and crowds flocked to hear him. He even played at the court of the Austrian empress in 1762 and met the six-year-old Marie Antoinette. By the age of eleven, Mozart was already an accomplished composer and had written three symphonies. He lived for a time in Paris but no one knows if Mozart and the Chevalier de Saint-George ever actually met. Mozart died penniless in Vienna at the age of thirty-five but left to the world some of the greatest music ever written. LEFT: Some of Mozart's original compositions.

In January of 1789, the queen came to see Saint-George give another kind of performance.

She watched from the shore as he did jumps and spins on skates before a crowd on a frozen pond at Versailles.

But it was the last time that Joseph would see Marie Antoinette. Only a few months later, ugly caricatures of the queen would be scrawled on walls in Paris. Nearby would be the words *Liberté! Egalité! Fraternité!* (Liberty! Equality! Brotherhood!) Ordinary people in France had become fed up with the absolute power of the king and the privileges of the aristocracy. While poor people starved because of bad harvests, the queen continued her life of frivolous luxury. She had come to represent all that they hated.

In July of 1789, rioters stormed the Bastille prison, a despised symbol of royal power. In October, another angry mob invaded Versailles and brought the king and queen back to Paris where they were held under guard in the Tuileries Palace. What began with a riot had become a revolution.

Joseph knew that change was needed in France. And he strongly supported the French Revolution's ideals of liberty and equality. He decided to drop his title of chevalier and become only the plain Monsieur (Mr.) de Saint-George. When the new republic of France went to war with Austria in April of 1792, Joseph volunteered to fight. So did other men of color from France's colonies. Joseph took command of a troop of a thousand black soldiers that was known as the "Legion of Saint-George." He became the first black colonel in the French army and fought bravely with his soldiers during the battle of Lille in September 1792. For a time, he was a revolutionary hero—but he could never have imagined the changes that revolution would bring.

Revolution!

By 1787, the King of France was bankrupt. Providing troops for the American Revolution had been very costly. Versailles and his other palaces were expensive to maintain. And the extravagances of his wife didn't help matters. To increase taxes he needed the approval of the Estates General, a group of the people's representatives that hadn't met in over 170 years. By summoning this body of people together again, King Louis XVI unknowingly lit a fuse that would explode into revolution.

Louis XVI is forced to wear a revolutionary red cap by citizens who invaded the Tuileries Palace on June 20, 1792

Winter 1788 — Crop failures cause food shortages in France. A story circulates that when the queen is told the people have no bread, she replies, "Then let them eat cake." Although Marie Antoinette never actually said this, she was believed to be a frivolous, selfish woman who manipulated her weak husband.

May 5, 1789 — The Estates General meets at Versailles and a bitter struggle breaks out between the representatives of the ordinary people and the officials of the aristocracy and the church. The elected deputies of the common people form their own group and demand a constitution for France. This group evolves into a National Constituent Assembly, which the king is grudgingly forced to accept.

July 14, 1789 — A Parisian crowd seizes the Bastille prison, kills its governor, and parades his severed head around the city.

August 4, 1789 — After angry uprisings by peasant farmers, the National Assembly agrees to abolish the feudal system which had kept peasants in bondage to wealthy landowners. On August 26, it passes the Declaration of the Rights of Man, which proclaims liberty and equality for all.

October 5, 1789 — When the king refuses to sign both of these decrees, angry Parisians march on Versailles. A mob invades the royal apartments looking to kill the queen. She escapes but her bed is slashed by swords and axes. The next day the royal family returns to Paris.

The attack on the Bastille on July 14, 1789

July 14, 1790
A huge festival is held in Paris commemorating the anniversary of the fall of the Bastille. The king and queen attend reluctantly, and Louis XVI takes an oath of loyalty to the new constitution.

June 20, 1791
The royal family tries to flee the country but is stopped at Varenne. They are returned to Paris where they are kept under close guard at the Tuileries Palace.

April 20, 1792
France declares war on Austria. Marie Antoinette's brother is now the emperor of Austria and an enemy of France.

August 10, 1792
As enemy forces enter France, many Parisians believe that the king and queen have betrayed them. A mob attacks the Tuileries Palace and the royal family is taken away and imprisoned.

September 21, 1792
After foreign forces are repelled, the monarchy is abolished and France is declared a republic.

January 21, 1793
Louis XVI is executed by guillotine in a public square in Paris. Alone in prison, Marie Antoinette awaits her fate.

O heavenly guillotine
You shorten kings and queens...

Songs about the guillotine were popular in Paris in 1793.

On October 16 of that year, Marie Antoinette was taken by cart from a prison cell to a large square in Paris named *Place de la Révolution.* Ahead of her, on a platform stained with blood, stood a tall, wooden rectangle with a heavy blade at the top of it. Nine months before, this guillotine had beheaded her husband. Now, she, too, was about to die.

As the shuddering blade dropped, the crowd roared. The executioner reached down for the severed head, grabbing it by the hair in which diamonds had once sparkled. He held it high to cheers of "*Vive la République!*" ("Long live the republic!")

But Joseph was not among the crowd that saw the queen die that day. He was in Lille, far away from Paris.

And he, too, was in danger of losing his head to the guillotine.

LEFT: This model of a guillotine shows the raised blade at the top. The condemned person lay face down on the bench and his neck was placed within the round yoke. When the blade was dropped, it sliced through the neck and the head fell into a waiting basket. This machine was invented in 1790 by Dr. Joseph Guillotin as a humane method of execution.

ABOVE: *At ten o'clock on the morning of October 16, 1793, the executioner arrived at Marie Antoinette's prison cell. He told her to hold out her hands so that he could tie her wrists. She objected and he roughly tied her hands behind her back. Then he cut her hair to the nape of her neck. Her husband had been taken to the guillotine in a coach—but she was put into a farm cart called a tumbril. The former queen stared silently ahead as the tumbril was pulled through the streets lined with people. As she climbed the steps to the scaffold, she stumbled and stepped on the executioner's foot. "Pardon, Monsieur," she said. "I did not do it on purpose." These were her last words.*

Six weeks before the queen was executed, the Reign of Terror had begun. An extremist faction led by a man named Robespierre had seized control of France's revolutionary government. Robespierre saw traitors to the revolution everywhere. Former aristocrats were particularly suspicious. Joseph was accused of stealing money that was meant for the men of his regiment. He was relieved of his command and then arrested and imprisoned. And he was not alone. During Robespierre's regime, over 300,000 people were arrested and 17,000 of them were sent to the guillotine.

For almost a year, Joseph shivered in a damp, cold cell wondering each morning if this day would be his last. Finally, in July of 1794, Robespierre was overthrown and the Reign of Terror came to an end. Fittingly, its leaders, including Robespierre, were sent to the guillotine. But Joseph remained in prison. His friends wrote letters to members of the new government asking that he be set free. "All the accusations against him are untrue," they stated. At last, on October 24, 1794, he was released from his jail cell.

RIGHT: Maximilien Robespierre was nicknamed "the Incorruptible" for his total devotion to the French Revolution. He was a leader of an extreme group called the Jacobins that came to power in September 1793. Robespierre and his followers believed that harsh measures were needed to save France from its enemies. But as the pace of the beheadings by the guillotine grew faster and faster, Robespierre's political rivals began plotting his overthrow. The tide turned against him and on July 27, 1794, he was shot in the jaw by a policeman trying to arrest him. The next day he was sent to the guillotine while the crowd shouted "Death to the tyrant!"

A year later the roles were reversed—the French government needed help from Monsieur de Saint-George. During the revolution, slavery had been outlawed but the revolutionary spirit had spread to France's colonies. In 1791, the former slaves on the island of Saint-Domingue (now Haiti) had risen up and taken over most of the plantations. They had rallied behind a dynamic black leader, the son of a slave, named Toussaint L'Ouverture. Toussaint wanted Saint-Domingue to be governed by him but protected by France.

The famous Saint-George was famous in the Caribbean as well. Would he consent, French officials asked, to meet with Toussaint and assess the situation in Saint-Domingue? And so, in the spring of 1796, Joseph stood on the deck of a sailing ship and breathed in the tropical scents of the green islands he had known as a boy.

Toussaint greeted Joseph and the other French representatives on board their ship in the harbor. He told them that he was fighting a rebellion led by a rival leader named Rigaud. In the months that Joseph and his committee were there, Rigaud's followers massacred many people. Joseph narrowly escaped being killed himself. Weary of violence and human cruelty, he boarded a ship for France in February of 1797.

LEFT: In 1801, Toussaint L'Ouverture united the island of Saint-Domingue and freed the slaves. But in January of 1802, Napoleon Bonaparte sent an army to invade Saint-Domingue. He wanted to restore slavery and return the island to being a colony. After some furious fighting, Toussaint agreed to a truce if the French would promise not to restore slavery. The French general agreed. But a few weeks later, Toussaint was captured and shipped off to prison in France, where he died on April 7, 1803. Napoleon tried to bring back slavery in Saint-Domingue but the Haitians rose up in defiance. On January 1, 1804, Haiti achieved independence, becoming the first black republic in history.

Back in Paris, Saint-George sought out the musicians he had once known. He was happy to find that many had survived the revolution and soon he began conducting his own orchestra once again. But Joseph was now a man in his fifties. And war and revolution had aged him. He lived alone in a small apartment in Paris and no longer danced the night away at fashionable parties.

One warm July day in 1798, an excited crowd gathered in the Monceau Park in Paris. Above their heads hovered a giant hot-air balloon—the latest sensation.

Posters announced that the balloonist was going to take a beautiful young girl aloft with him.

"Oh, and there she is! And who is that man with her?" murmured people in the crowd. "Why, it's the famous Saint-George! He's still alive!"

People cheered as Joseph promenaded around the park with the young lady on his arm. Joseph helped the beautiful girl into the basket below the balloon and then watched as it floated aloft. Soon, the balloon was just a dot in the blue sky.

RIGHT: A hot-air balloon takes flight over the palace of the Tuileries on September 19, 1784. The experiments of two brothers, Joseph and Etienne Montgolfier, had led to the creation of the first hot-air balloons. On September 19, 1783, they conducted a demonstration at Versailles and sent a sheep, a duck, and a rooster aloft. By November of that year, two men were brave enough to go up in a balloon, becoming the world's first aerial pilots.

But this was to be Saint-George's last public appearance. A few months later, he complained of stomach pains. On June 10, 1799, he died from an acute ulcer in his liver. The newspapers that had once praised his music, noted his passing with respect. In a world where black people could hope to be little more than servants, Joseph Bologne, Monsieur de Saint-George, had become one of the most dazzling and celebrated men of his time.

For most of the next two centuries, Saint-George was almost forgotten. But in recent years, musicians have rediscovered his music. Concerts are being given and recordings made. An opera about his life was performed in 2005 in France. A street in Paris has been named for him.

But the best monument to Joseph Bologne, Chevalier de Saint-George, is his music. In its slower, quieter moments we hear the loneliness of a black man in a white world. And in its lively, quick-tempoed passages, we can see the agility of the champion fencer and imagine the elegance and style that charmed the queen of France.

The famous Saint-George is famous once again.

44

Author's Note

I first heard about the Chevalier de Saint-George on the radio. The announcer briefly described the Chevalier's remarkable life and then played his Second Violin Concerto. I found myself humming the sparkling tune from the Rondo while I worked. The same tune captured me once again during a television program about the life of Saint-George, called *Le Mozart Noir: Reviving a Legend*. This led me to Alain Guédé's *Monsieur de Saint-George*, (St. Martin's, 2003), the only biography of the Chevalier in English. It is a colorful and engaging account that encouraged me to think that young readers, too, might be interested in Saint-George's story. I'm grateful to Alain Guédé for the many scenes from the life of Saint-George that he evokes so effectively. Since the Chevalier's life and music have been rediscovered only recently, research by historians continues to uncover new information. I'm indebted to a book recently published in France entitled *Le Chevalier de Saint-George* by Claude Ribbe (Éditions Perrin, 2005) that contains new information about the Chevalier's early life and gives him a different year of birth—and even a different father—from Alain Guédé's account. For these details I have relied on Professor Ribbe's research. Other selected references are listed on page 46 but I would like to note that *The Grove Dictionary of Music* and Britannica Online were helpful throughout. I would also like to acknowledge my editor, Tamar Brazis, and designer, Celina Carvalho, as well as Beverly Slopen and Catherine Lapautre.

Bibliography

Dunlap, Ian. *Marie-Antoinette*. London: Sinclair-Stevenson, 1993.

Erickson, Carolly. *To the Scaffold: The Life of Marie Antoinette*. New York: W. Morrow, 1991.

Gay, Peter. *Mozart*. New York: Viking, 1999.

Guédé, Alain. *Monsieur de Saint-George*. New York: St. Martin's, 2003.

Hibbert, Christopher. *The Days of the French Revolution*. London: Penguin, 1982.

Isaacson, Walter. *Benjamin Franklin*. New York: Simon & Schuster, 2003.

Lever, Evelyne. *Marie Antoinette*. New York: Farrar, Straus and Giroux, 2000.

Myers, Walter Dean. *Toussaint L'Ouverture*. New York: Simon & Schuster, 1996.

Parkinson, Wanda. *"This Gilded African": Toussaint L'Ouverture*. London: Quartet Books, 1980.

Ribbe, Claude. *Le Chevalier de Saint-George*. Paris: Perrin, 2004.

Schama, Simon. *Citizens: A Chronicle of the French Revolution*. New York: Knopf, 1989.

Wenborn, Neil. *Joseph Haydn*. London: Pavilion, 1997.

Quotation Credits

Page 11: "Perhaps the most extraordinary man…" La Boëssière's son was a lifelong friend of Saint-George. In 1818, he described Joseph in his preface to his *Treatise on the Art of Weapons*. The quotations on page 12 (caption) are also from this source as cited in Alain Guédé's *Monsieur de Saint-George*.

Page 12: "two rows of pearls" from *Mémoires* by Madame de Genlis, as cited by Alain Guédé. "Oh the joy of being loved tenderly…" is from a song with music by Saint-George entitled "The Other Day Beneath the Trees."

Page 15: Excerpt from John Adams's diary as cited by Claude Ribbe in *Le Chevalier de Saint-George*.

Page 16: "Sacrifices to politics." From a letter by Maria-Theresa as cited in *Marie Antoinette* by Evelyn Lever.

Page 17: "Vive Franklin!", cited in *Benjamin Franklin* by Walter Isaacson.

Page 25: "Subject to the orders of a mulatto." The letter was quoted in the correspondence of the Baron de Grimm, 1752, as cited by Alain Guédé.

Page 36: "O heavenly guillotine…" This song was sung to the tune of the "Marseillaise," as cited by Alain Guédé.

Page 37: "Pardon, monsieur…" as reported by the Paris newspaper *Moniteur* cited by Christopher Hibbert in *The Days of the French Revolution*.

Page 38: "All the accusations…" is a summary of what was said in many letters sent in Saint-George's defense, as cited by Claude Ribbe.

Glossary

cabriolet: a light, two-wheeled carriage drawn by one horse.

concerto: a musical composition for one or more soloists and orchestra.

constitution: a document that states the way in which a country is organized and its laws applied.

crème de la crème: a French expression meaning the best of the best.

chevalier: a French title that would be the same as a knighthood in England.

dauphin: the oldest son (prince) of a king of France.

dauphine: the wife of the dauphin.

empress: the female ruler of an empire or the wife of an emperor.

feudal: a system in Europe during medieval times where tenant farmers lived and worked lands owned by lords who were their masters. Much of this system had survived in France into the 1700s.

guillotine: a machine used for beheading by means of a heavy sliding blade. It was invented as a humane form of execution by Dr. Louis Guillotin and first used in 1792. The guillotine was last used in France in 1977.

half-caste: a term used for a person of mixed racial descent that is today considered derogatory.

hameau: A hamlet or small village. Marie Antoinette's *hameau* can still be seen at Versailles today.

lady in waiting: an aristocratic woman who served as an attendant to a queen or princess in a royal household.

midwife: a woman who assists other women in childbirth.

mulatto: an outdated name for someone with both black and white parents that is today considered offensive.

parry: to block or ward off a blow in fencing.

quartet: a musical composition for four instruments or voices.

touche: (pronounced *toosh*) a French word used for a hit in fencing.

Recommended Discs

Le Mozart Noir, Tafelmusik, Jeanne Lamon, CBC Records.
Saint-Georges: Violin Concertos Volumes 1 and 2, Toronto Camerata, Naxos Records.
Chevalier de Saint-George: String Quartets Op.14, Apollon String Quartet; Avenira Records.

Haydn: 6 Paris Symphonies, Berlin Philharmonic, Herbert von Karajan; Deutsche Grammophon Masters.
Le Mozart Noir DVD, Award-winning film, CBC Opening Night.

For my mother — H.B.

For the remarkable and inspiring Joseph Bologne, the Chevalier de Saint-George — E.V.

Picture Credits

Page 1: National Portrait Gallery, London; **Page 4:** Schomburg Center / Art Resource, NY; **Page 6-7:** Bridgeman-Giraudon / Art Resource, NY; **Page 10:** Victoria & Albert Museum, London / Art Resource, NY; **Page 11:** *Old Sword Play*, by Alfred Hutton / Toronto Public Library; **Page 13:** Fine Art Photographic Library, London / Art Resource, NY; **Page 14:** National Portrait Gallery, Smithsonian Institution / Art Resource, NY; **Page 18:** (top) Bildarchiv Preussischer Kulturbesitz / Art Resource, NY, (bottom) Erich Lessing / Art Resource, NY; **Page 20:** Réunion des Musées Nationaux / Art Resource, NY; **Page 22:** Erich Lessing / Art Resource, NY; **Page 23:** Réunion des Musées Nationaux / Art Resource, NY;

Page 24: Réunion des Musées Nationaux / Art Resource, NY; **Page 25:** The New York Public Library / Art Resource, NY; **Page 27:** Mary Evans Picture Library; **Page 28:** Erich Lessing / Art Resource, NY; **Page 30:** Erich Lessing / Art Resource, NY; **Page 31:** (top) Erich Lessing / Art Resource, NY, (bottom) Erich Lessing / Art Resource, NY; **Page 34:** Mary Evans Picture Library; **Page 35:** Bridgeman-Giraudon / Art Resource, NY; **Page 36:** Bridgeman-Giraudon / Art Resource, NY; **Page 37:** Erich Lessing / Art Resource, NY; **Page 38:** Bridgeman-Giraudon / Art Resource, NY; **Page 41:** Bridgeman-Giraudon / Art Resource, NY; **Page 43:** Réunion des Musées Nationaux / Art Resource, NY.

Design by Celina Carvalho
Production Manager: Alexis Mentor

Library of Congress Cataloging-in-Publication Data:
Brewster, Hugh.
The other Mozart : the life of the famous Chevalier de Saint-George / by Hugh Brewster ; illustrated by Eric Velasquez.
p. cm.
ISBN 13: 978-0-8109-5720-6
ISBN 10: 0-8109-5720-5
1. Saint-Georges, Joseph Boulogne, chevalier de, d. 1799—Juvenile literature. 2. Musicians—France—Biography—Juvenile literature. 3. Racially mixed people—France—Biography—Juvenile literature. 4. Nobility—France—Biography—Juvenile literature. I. Velasquez, Eric, ill. II. Title.

ML3930.S13B74 2006
944'.004960092—dc22

2006007488

Text copyright © 2007 Hugh Brewster
Original illustrations copyright © 2007 Eric Velasquez

Printed and bound in China
10 9 8 7 6 5 4 3 2 1

HNA
harry n. abrams, inc.
a subsidiary of La Martinière Groupe

115 West 18th Street
New York, NY 10011
www.hnabooks.com